The Ramblings of a Travelling Man

Anthony Wilkins

The Ramblings of a Travelling Man
Anthony Wilkins © 2021

First Published by Compass-Publishing UK
ISBN - 978-1-913713-39-3

Cover photo © Terry Wilkins
Photos © Anthony Wilkins and Victoria White
Typeset by The Book Refinery Ltd
www.thebookrefinery.com

Disclaimer
All poems are the work of the author.
Any similarity to real persons, living or dead, is coincidental and
not intended by the author.

Printed and bound by CMP (UK) Dorset

In Memoriam

Bro. *The Revd Doctor,*

Peter Johnson

Grand Chaplain for the Province of Cornwall 2018

This book of verse is dedicated to the memory of our brother, the Reverend Doctor Peter Johnson.

It was at Peter's Third degree festive board that I read out my first creation relating to Freemasonry. The poem entitled 'The Third' is a verse for each degree a Freemason undertakes on his path towards being raised to the sublime degree of Master Mason.

Brother Peter was initiated, passed and raised in Penwith Lodge No 8538 in the Province of Cornwall under the United Grand Lodge of England.

In exceedingly short order, his worth was noted by the Province and he was offered the position of Provincial Grand Chaplain for the Province of Cornwall. Peter accepted the honour of this office and was invested in 2018.

Sadly, tragedy was to strike later in the year when Peter was diagnosed with a particularly aggressive form of cancer, a disease he fought valiantly with true strength, stoicism and faith. But he inevitably lost this battle, leaving a huge hole in the hearts of all who were privileged to have known or spent time with him.

Few people encountered in life, especially for such a short time as I knew Peter, will leave such a lasting impression. His memory lives on in our hearts and minds as he undoubtedly goes on, having ascended to the Grand Lodge above, where the Lord calls home those deserving to bask in the glory of his favour and grace.

FOREWORD

David Maskell

I am writing this Foreword in the middle of one of the worst pandemics the world has encountered, at a time when everyone is looking for a little hope and inspiration.

Having celebrated the tercentenary of Freemasonry in 2017, we are now facing the longest period of abstinence from our meetings that most of us will have known.

It is therefore a comforting reminder of better times to read this collection of Masonic rhymes and to remind ourselves of the strengths, values and friendships that first attracted us to the Order.

I first encountered Ant's poetry towards the end of 2019 and, since that time, whenever anything of note has occurred within the Province, Ant has always had a suitable poem ready – to entertain and inspire.

This book has involved a tremendous amount of work by Ant, not just in the creative processes of writing but also in trying to achieve his aim of seeing his work published. The poems draw on his experiences whilst serving in the forces and also his strong commitment to Freemasonry.

I hope that when you read these poems, they will help you to reflect on what Freemasonry means to you, to remember the reasons why you joined the Order and that they will inspire us all to better things.

I commend this collection to you, whether a Freemason or not. I hope you will enjoy reading it as much as I did and that it will provide hope and encouragement to us all for the future.

W. Bro David G. Maskell. PSGD. Assistant Provincial Grand Master

CONTENTS

POEMS

INTRODUCTION

Freemasonry is at the heart of how many brothers conduct their lives. Some will attend one lodge regularly and visit others; some will join numerous lodges and maybe progressive orders. What Freemasonry actually means or represents is for each brother, male or female, depending on their Grand Lodge jurisdiction, to ascertain for themselves as they interpret the ritual and tenets over time.

One thing we all act on are the principles of brotherly love, relief and truth. These go hand in hand with the key points we explore constantly of integrity, friendship, respect and charity.

It is with these points in mind that I have created this book of my poetry for your enjoyment. I hope you do enjoy the words, rhyme and the sentiment behind those words, and understand, even if you have a differing viewpoint from my interpretation, the meaning conveyed in these works regarding Freemasonry.

Please accept my thanks for each and every brother, or curious non-Mason, who has purchased a copy to collectively contribute to the great charitable work we all continue to carry out. A percentage of the profit from this book will be deposited into the Masonic Charitable Foundation to be faithfully applied to a myriad of worthy causes.

I leave you with two quotes from one of the most famous Freemasons of modern times, Sir Winston Churchill:

'The true guide of life is to do what is right.'

'We make a living by what we get, but we make a life by what we give!'

May God, the Great Architect of the Universe, bless and keep you and your families in high spirits and good health.

Bro Anthony Wilkins,

Penwith Lodge 8538
Millennium Lodge 9708
Lodge of the Chisel 9398

In the Province of Cornwall, under the United Grand Lodge of England.

KEEP

CALM

AND

REMEMBER

YOU ARE A

FREEMASON

Tercentennial Ode

Our fraternity is older, that which we hold dear
And we have celebrated our three hundredth year.
Of the Grand Lodge of England, strong and stable,
Built on foundations, of our past, so ancient become fable.

The path was set and story laid down so,
Our ritual teaches us this, with our tales of woe.
The secrets were lost, because of those with naught
To find them again we travel as taught.

Secrets replaced with others, maybe new,
Signs and tokens and a grip so true,
We travel, befriend, assist and do right,
Charity in the name of the Great Architect, whilst searching more light.

But times have caught us and in years maybe few,
The fraternity expanded and lodges all grew.
Meetings held, and decisions made,
Regularity and order, and rules to aid.

The creation of a Grand Lodge, uniting those from before,
It has stood the test of time, of that we are sure.
Years of a hundred, centuries times three,
Belonging to this, my brothers, matters to me.

Proud and tall, we no longer hide,
The world now knows our charitable side.
Masons we are, accepted and free,
And we are proud to have celebrated our Tercentenary.

Our Ladies of Lodge

Our ladies are those women,
We as Masons hold close.
They support our every challenge,
For they are surely better than most.

To our lodge we dedicate time,
And to charity some of our pay.
Our wonderful ladies uphold and promote this,
Promoting betterment of their man each day.

Freemasonry is rumoured to make good men better,
From the invitation to join the lodge in a letter.
Our ladies are always with us, oft sharing our Masonic path,
Because of that gift of love, men and women in God's good grace shall have.

The first sign of madness, is said to be talking to one's self,
Our other halves humour this, instead of questioning our health.
The ladies leave us carrying on, smile and often help as we plan,
Help hosting a lodge function, or organising with us, as they can.

We mumble our plans and ritual, and all those cursed lines,
They know that much is a secret, and do not press us on those signs.
Our ladies ignore the words they think they should maybe not hear,
But that knowing nod of encouragement allays many a fine brother's fear.

We enjoy our lodges, whilst they may enjoy some peace,
They do their own thing, whilst we partake of many a fine feast.
But there does arise opportunity to include our ladies too,
And in the grand scheme of life, without the ladies,
We couldn't give Freemasonry its due.

So, this wee story is for our ladies: girlfriends, mums, daughters or partners,
And for those of us who are wed, the commanding title of wives.
Without your indefatigable support of our endeavours,
We could not travel this Masonic path in our lives.

AND I SAY AGAIN –

Our ladies are those women,
We as Masons hold close.
They support our every challenge,
For they are surely better than most.

The 'Weight' of Masonry

Some talk of me being a Mason,
Whilst others don't really care.

Some accuse me of keeping torrid secrets,
Whilst others look at my badge or ring, snigger and stare.

I know the truth! And I'm proud as hell.
I love being a Mason, and to all, I'll admit or tell.

But what do I get out of it?
If you like I will share:

With all those meetings and fine food,
All I really get, in my trousers, is a tear!

17

The Masonic Traveller

By bus or car, of air and by train,
We travel the world over, destination the same.
To visit another lodge, whilst searching more light,
Along the way meeting our brethren, making friends each night.

From hamlets and villages, towns and cities, we come to meet you,
Visiting, at the heart of Freemasonry, a great thing we fraternally do.
Enjoying differences, in ritual and workings, that of course can oft be found,
Cementing and sharing enjoyment, in the love of our craft so profound.

We give our time, our love, and to charity from our pockets deep.
The Lord taught us to be our brother's keeper, a sense of fulfilment being
the profit we reap.
A Freemason's love for his brothers, and of society as a whole,
Presses him to travel, his journey enlightening, thus filling up his soul.

The travelling man, with ritual saved within his Masonic head,
Searches genuine secrets lost, because of an evil act that slew
our master dead.
King Solomon's decree was we travel, and with brothers we always meet,
Strengthening Masonic bonds of each brother beside us,
perched upon his seat.
In modern times symbolically, in case the true never reappear,
The travelling man enjoys both learning and meeting,
As he visits his brothers, year upon year.

The Privilege of a Lewis

My son is a Lewis, and this by my design,
He is so because of me, in my supplication to the architect divine.
A young man emulates his elders, and father most of all.
He learns to be an asset to society and humanity all.

As he nears an age where he is considered mature,
If he holds true to taught ideals, he may be offered the same chance for sure.
From boy to man, he watched his ole dad,
Oft dressed up and gone all night – it sometimes made him sad.

As he grew up, he asked his dad why,
Of all the nights away, that sometimes made him cry.
My son, let me teach you, how we as men can be good;
Give to charity, serve society, but have fun, as of course you should.

Stories how Masons make a difference, and how it's all worked,
In the news he sees the same, knowing his dad hasn't shirked.
Learning that time away was oft well spent,
He accepts our sacrifice, so less and less he'll lament.

Part of the teachings I have imparted to him:
Importance of family – to aid them not is committing a sin.
Assisting in age his dear mum and dad,
He proves a stout fellow, as taught, and makes us glad.

To take the weight and render his father ease,
Perhaps more symbolically, or speculatively, could appease.
By birth, free and accepted, by actions, certain privilege may be bestowed,
To welcome a Lewis to lodge, before all others, is the course of this ode.

A man he has become, more than any son is this one, my Lewis,
I wish him to follow my regular steps, and through the rites, he can do this.
From relationship of father and son, we add a new one, yes another,
My Lewis, my boy, as a man, may become my brother!

Our Almoner

There is a brother in lodge who we all know and love,
For him, his calling is to help all, and he can never do enough.
He shares our woes, and reports on those in need,
He rallies all brethren to help if they can, with all haste and speed.

Constant contact with families of those who've lost the most,
Some brothers sadly gone, but family still included, as he keeps his post.
Presents and invites are oft given, inclusivity the way he sets his stall,
The office of Almoner is one of those, dedicated to help all.

He makes his reports in lodge, a small act for his part.
But we should realise, this is only the end, a continuation, or the start
Of the time and effort, our brother puts in;
Acts of selflessness and charity for the good of us all, and also if needed,
our kin.

Dedication to the fraternity, families, in all Masonic traits and specifically
of welfare,
His course is steadfast, he is a brother, whose motto is to care.
I purport in our lodges, the Almoner should be supported,
praised like numerous others,
For he is surely one of our most valued, compassionate,
and hard-working brothers!

The Candidate

The candidate is a friend, a mate, a pal and a bud,
He asked a few questions, showing interest as one should.
The chats have turned serious, after some light-hearted play,
In your Mason's mind, the conscience or inner voice had something to say.

This man is a friend, you're close; almost a brother, you could purport.
His heart is charitable, an upstanding man, jolly and a good sort.
My friend has proven to me, the qualities of Masonic thread,
But there's that voice, whispering inside my head.

Should I ask him, as he hasn't asked me?
Should I leave it and let things be?
I think he would like to, and my question be heard –
No, he's just an interested mate; don't be absurd.
And then it was my turn to act as I should,
To give him the chance – would he join if he could?

'My friend, can I talk to you seriously? A question if you care:
Would you like to join us, and act as a brother on the square?
I can tell you little, but am sure you're the sort.
Truly a fine fellow; mature, and of good report.'

He replied, 'What an honour, to brotherhood and charity, I acquiesce.'
And now he is here, he answered well, you can surely guess.
He knows little of the order, but conscience suggested that he should,
And tonight he joined, right where he stood.

In our temple up yonder, he went through the rite.
He has been balloted, approved, and initiated this night.
My brothers, I give you the candidate.
A friend, a mate, a pal and a bud.
Now let me amend those phrases, as you know I should.
In a meek and mild manner, he acted as many another.
On this night I present to you my brethren – OUR BROTHER.

The Third

I once was in darkness, devoid of light.
Then was initiated, with a feeling of fright.
Humbled by dress, words and deed,
It had taken root, this Masonic seed.
A journey to be travelled, guided, by learned others,
This is more than a club, a society of brothers.
'But why do it?' some Cowan would ask.
To explain then, was some task.
The answer is vague, a feeling inside;
I knew the answer, but was tongue-tied.
I worried over belonging, in this new fraternity of friends.
A close-knit brethren, on whom I hoped I could depend.

Then came the second, passed one night.
After learning some questions, I answered them right.
I felt a belonging and started to progress,
The mystery still there, but I felt no stress.
More questions were given and again I learned,
Because the ritual is fun, and for knowledge I yearned.
A Fellowcraft then, charity my task,
'But why do it?' some Cowan would still ask.
My answer was then taking more form.
As I learnt some more, I ignored the scorn.
To the uninitiated I try to say,
I am travelling a path and finding my way.
I felt a belonging, in this fraternity of friends.
A close-knit brethren, on whom I was sure I could depend.

And now time has gone by and it is still fun.
I have learnt so much, with more yet to come.
I feel elated and am not fazed,
For on this night I have been raised.
The mystery remains and interest never wanes,
Dedication to lodge; my brothers, are much the same.
We speak of words, signs, tools, and a grip with our hand,
Let us not slip, fellow masters, we all understand!
An obligation, an oath we took.
But here comes that question, again, yet look.
'But why do it?' a Cowan will ask.
The answer is now, an easier task.
To the uninitiated I stand and say,
I am travelling a path and finding my way.
I am a Master Mason.
A brother, in this fraternity of friends.
A close-knit brethren, on whom I know I can always depend.

The Masonic Sacrifice

In time of war so great, when all are embroiled,
The duty of our countrymen to volunteer and become soiled.
As men of honour, free, accepted and true,
Among them, brothers and masons volunteer to see it through.

In fields of the Second, and trenches of the First,
Masons were involved, whilst war waged its worst.
Fighting on land or sea, and also in the air,
Tales of derring-do, they fought for what's fair.

They fell in their thousands, alongside brothers in blood,
Duty to country, Masonic ideals, fulfilled as one should.
The horrors of war become a tale to be told,
Sacrifice of countrymen and Masons, all so bold.

In the month of November, on Armistice Day,
We remember the fallen, and brothers this way:
In services, parades, and odes so true;
For our countrymen and Freemason Brothers –
Our eternal thanks belong to you.

Grace

Initiate

Lord, we thank you for this feast, after initiating our new brother.
You bless us with sustenance, and by filling our ranks with another.
For the food we eat,
And the brothers we meet,
May we be ever thankful.
Amen.

General Meetings

Lord our God, the creator of all,
Your teachings keep us steadfast, where others may fall.
For this gift of food, and also fine wine,
Our thanks be to you, oh architect divine.
Amen.

General Meetings

Our Lord God above, who provides our food, scoff or scran,
You bless us with fine food, every brother to a man.
We thank you for the favour to us that you give,
We accept that which you deliver to enable us to live.
Whilst we eat this eve, and our bellies make full,
We sing silent praise, to the creator of all.
Amen.

Burns Grace

Oh Lord of all, the provider of sustenance and subject of our faith,
On this memorial night of our brother and poet, Rabbie Burns,
We thank you for the food for which each belly yearns.
The neeps, tatties and haggis, which our hunger will sate,
We owe to you, the Great Architect and inspiration of our brother,
the Poet Laureate.
Amen.

Installation

Lord, our creator, on this Installation night,
We give thanks for this feast, after performing our ritual right.
We are thankful for our brothers, who share with us this eve;
It is to you we owe our all, for what we are about to receive.
Amen.

Prayers After Festive Boards

Initiation

Lord, we thank you for this feast, which our hunger did sate.
By your grace, we dine and welcome new brothers,
But as we feel full, may we remember the needs of others.
Amen.

Installation

Lord, we thank you for this installation feast, which our hunger did sate.
By your grace, we dined, taking our fill from each plate.
We give thanks for this meal with our brothers,
But as we feel full, may we always remember the needs of others.
Amen.

General

Lord, as Solomon ordered, we travelled and have now dined.
It is in your good grace and favour, we ourselves believe we find.
We give thanks for the meal at our table, which you did bring,
And vow to assist others likewise, to aid them in their suffering.
Amen.

A Toast to the Province

Worshipful Master, Provincial Grand Master, Grand Officers, Provincial
Grand Officers, Distinguished Brethren, Brethren All.

It is sometimes described a duty, but nay, it is an honour to
propose this toast.
Those we know and appreciate, some may be closer than most.
To raise a glass to our brethren is befitting of a perfect host,
And is certainly welcomed after such a fine roast.

I already go on, as this night is fading fast,
Brethren below those aforementioned ranks, be upstanding
[pause for movement]
As we toast the Provincial Grand Officers, both present and past.

Beat of the Masonic Heart

Our heart beats within our body,
A thunder within our chest.
But mine is the heart of a Mason,
By trials and approbation, by examination, it has been put unto the test.

I was intrigued – a lodge and fraternity I joined.
I worked my way through each Masonic degree.
Developing and making myself better.
For this I am a fitter member of society, I hope you can all agree.

For betterment of myself and my brothers, through faith and charity,
Is the method by which I toil.
Serving my brothers and fellow man,
An honourable lifestyle, from which no one could recoil.

My life continues as before,
I still make mistakes, and myself I sometimes detest.
But with guidance from our fraternity and ritual, I stand and try again;
Do what I can for the good of all, and in this I shall never rest!

As the years go by, my blood cools, I become the man that I want.
Fewer mistakes, more learned; and could even be described as wise.
It is largely down to the support and all the learning
Of Freemasonry, my brothers, that we all brought into our lives.

Intellect rules our actions and thoughts.
This is tempered, symbolically, by what is in our heart.
When times are hard, and I feel my back is up against the wall,
Masonic ideals ensure that, with candour, once again I shall restart.

Freemasonry defines us as good and charitable men,
Maybe no different from many others.
But my heart tells me it means more,
Because we belong to a society of brothers.

Our hearts beat within our bodies,
Imbued with Masonic ideal, thunderous within our chests.
Believe that this is our defining glory,
To withstand any tribulations that in our life can be seen as tests.

Master of the Lodge

The brother in the big seat is the master of the lodge.
He represents the brethren with candour and his duty, he does not dodge.
It can be ritual heavy, pure enormity of a task.
He remains calm and collected, his face full of confidence, a perfect mask.

He rules the lodge in a firm but fun, and inclusive way;
At each festive board, many a kind word, our visitors have to say.
Of his preparation for, and dedication to performing the ritual right,
To watch him work is to behold a fine sight.

It takes a good few years until you occupy King Solomons' chair.
Time well spent learning the craft; to get there too fast would not
seem so fair.
And now he sits there, commanding in his place,
Pride in his lodge, reflected by brethren, on each and every face.

*Worshipful Master, we aspire in time to follow your lead,
For in our candidates, and progressive offices,
your example sows a fine seed.
Exemplifying, as a Freemason, the way in which to conduct oneself,
In the prestigious office you hold, we oft toast your performance; and, of
course, your health.

The humble representative of King Solomon, and our master Hiram Abiff,
The Worshipful Master's place is a blessing,
And to us, my brethren, the Great Architect's latest gift!

*[Insert Worshipful Bro. name if appropriate]

A Burns Memory

On the 25th of January, we celebrate and remember each year,
Paying homage to our Poet Laureate's memory, which so many hold dear.
We celebrate his life, and the work of such fine poetic art.
Though not all Scots, we do this, for as a Mason,
he holds a place in our heart.

His life beset with woes, Masonic influence exampled in his art,
Dedicated to the brothers of St James, as a Mason he played his part.
He thought to leave his Masonic mother to dwell on Jamaican soil.
His brothers bade him reconsider, and here he remained and
continued to toil.

With 'Ode to a Haggis', his work blessed a relation to food.
We do this still today, by grace before and after,
which without would be rude.
'Auld Lang Syne' presents, for mankind and his brothers, a feeling in the
soul at the deepest rung,
That we, as Freemasons, share with our brother, whether spoken or sung.

This eve we pay our respects, and remember our bard;
His work lightens up many a day, if a brother's life feels hard.
We remember him again, in this yet another year,
Our friend and brother, Robbie, of whom his memory is so dear.

A Masonic Week

Monday's Mason has his whole week planned.

Tuesday's Mason uses a diary, as he doesn't know offhand.

Wednesday's Mason travels, visiting brothers, from place to place.

Thursday's Mason is full from festive boards, evenings of stuffing his face!

Friday's Mason is glad of the weekend, and longs for it to begin.

Saturday's Mason is out again; his other half laments it's becoming a sin.

But the Mason who prays and practises ritual on the Sabbath day
Is set for the following week, where he again will go out to play!

Masonic Fire

There is a practice that is sometimes enacted
During the toasts, where some lodges do, and some have redacted.

A fun part of toasting, clapping, to catch each other out;
If you get it wrong there is some chortling, the odd fine,
and undoubted shout.

'Taking your time from me,' starts the firing cry,
Points left right, brothers follow suit, and must not act shy.

Firing in festive boards can add more to each Masonic toast.
In some lodges it adds a memorable difference and amusement,
after each and every roast.

Exaltation

Having been a Freemason for a good little while,
Initiated, passed and raised, stones passed figuratively as a landmark of each
Masonic mile.

Now ambitious to continue and progress within our wonderful craft,
A multitude of other orders, but which to choose from this
equally worthy raft?

Many brothers promoted Royal Arch as the fourth and natural next step.
I asked around and gained more insight, or as much as I could of course –
this was my prep.

And now I have joined the Holy Royal Arch chapter;
More regalia, ritual and learning, exalted that night with a feeling
of awe and rapture.

A new degree and a different but equally enjoyable new order,
The night began with feelings of trepidation,
like the proverbial lamb to the slaughter.

I now have more learning, and also wear a jewel, a kind of medallion;
Another moment in life where I feel so proud, as my brothers
call me a companion.

A Brother's Lament

The loss of a loved one
Is the hardest burden to bear.

All those years of love
Enjoyed without a care.

Signs of heartbreak and loss, clear for all to see,
Deep-seated emotion, like fabric, now symbolically bears a tear.

Brother, anything you need or small comfort I can give,
With my time I will gladly share.

In your time of distress, we offer this and more,
To show you that, in your darkest hours, we as brethren, really do care.

Then and Now

There is a time and a place in history, we as Masons oft tell,
Around its building, and those involved, our ritual explains so well.
The lives of those who went long before,
The woes that befell them, which we now travel to repair for sure.

The history of King Solomon and Hiram, our master,
is now but a tale to be told,
And through our ritual, in stages or degrees, it will symbolically unfold.
Representation of each Masonic journey, clearly for us to see,
Contemplating the days of old through fable, and in supplication,
as we take a knee.

Between the pillars and before sacred law we kneel,
as past brethren once did,
Making vows, oaths so solemn, ignoring those feelings of worry well rid!
Explanation of our rite is forthcoming to each new generation
Of those who came before; we act with the reverence due such veneration.

In times gone by, and now those in which we live,
Many things change, but then and now, to charity all Masons give.
A society of brothers, an order in which we all desire to remain,
Over the years many things changed, but then again,
many are still the same!

The Masonic Charity Festival

Every few years, Grand Lodge may make a decree:
For charity we make so much, but can we make more? Let us see.
A drive to, in a dedicated year, an indeterminate amount we can collect
And donate to worthy cause, our ideals fulfilled, or so we can reflect.

Charities of the order abound, merged all under one hat,
Easing control and speed of delivery, one could ask for no more than that.
Branded Masonic Charitable Fund, and for the festival of 2024,
Brothers work hard, with ideas or in support, raising more and more
and more.

We give or raise as much as we can, seeking naught for ourselves in return;
Knowledge that we have done our part to help, sincerely,
is our only concern.
'Who really benefits? Funding and providing for whom?'
we may want to know.
Anyone or any cause when in need; but there is, in fact,
a greater seed we sow.

As free and accepted brethren of the finest, most ancient fraternal order,
Our ritual and knowledge, encompassed by charity, as our figurative border;
To those in society who know little, or refuse to learn and accept,
We continue our good work regardless, earning many a Cowan's respect.

Through giving and charitable acts, we set the finest example,
Whether we give little as we are poor, or plenty, if we find in our
pockets ample.
And through exemplary conduct others may learn, and by invite or request,
May assist or be initiated, as we help, in them, to bring out their very best.

Brothers, let us pull together, we brethren of the mystic tie,
2024 is not so far away, and whilst we work so hard, time will certainly fly!
The Masonic Charity festival, culminating next in two thousand and
twenty-four –
Let us, my brothers, make this the greatest success yet; another one we can
again be thoroughly proud of for sure.

The University Scheme Creed

We are Freemasons of the University Scheme,
We will travel and search light, through the knowledge we glean.

We are part of the future; and long may it last,
We will honour our fraternity, and also the past.

Hiram, our Master; we will make him proud.
To those who would hear, we spread his word loud.

We will live by our order's principles and nurture this seed,
As University Scheme brethren, we swear, this is our creed!

Widows' Sons

Some brothers have common interests, oft forming a group or a body,
This ode is about a means of transport, a lifestyle, or for some, a hobby!

Brethren of the Widows' Sons, they combine their Masonic pride,
In our beloved fraternity, and the bikes that they ride.

Their camaraderie, charity, biker vests or 'cuts', the stuff of many a
brother's talk,
These men follow the same path; they are brothers who ride,
as well as walk!

Across the planet, at charity and biking events, you will hear their
powerful roar!
The revving engines of the Widows' Sons, our biker brothers on tour.

Silent Gavel

Our gavels are silent,
In safety, we're bid not to meet.
Soon enough, again we'll gather,
Once more each brother will take his temple seat.

This kind of silence happened before,
In another country, then due to Nazi rot.
Take comfort in the square and the compass,
And, of course, the forget-me-not.

This enforced abstinence,
Places masonry in our thoughts.
We look forward to seeing brothers once more,
When again, we will give and receive our reports!

Thoughts drift toward charity;
In our solitude, we plan, and ideas conceive:
What can we, as Freemasons, do,
To give others some brief reprieve?

In the name of the Great Architect,
Creator of all in this life,
We should all still do our best,
To relieve another's strife.

Masonic Secrets

Words, signs, tokens, and grips,
Taught in our ritual, to each and every one of you.
Sworn secrets, never to be shown or uttered, without caution,
Unless to another, you know to be a Mason true.

Freemasonry is not a secret society.
Instead, a society with 'secrets'; much can, and is,
made of that one simple word.
Conspiracy theorists jump on it: secrets! Or is that privacy?
Made abhorrent,

Twisting charity and goodwill into something malignant that shouldn't
be heard!
'You know that funny Mason handshake – is it under or over the leg?'
Questions like this, uttered by those not on the square.
We will not tell them, although to find out these days is simple;
We're discreet, wish to be better, something about which we care!

'Are your secret words a prayer; or maybe a curse?
While shaking each hand, do you twist, shake, then freeze?
Or is it that you do a jiggly dance, you know the one, behind closed doors,
With head between legs, whilst the knees give it a squeeze?'

Conspiracies about Masonry, sometimes amusing and light fun,
But there are those who defame, bitterly manipulating every word.
Charity and deeds forgotten, it's those secrets they think we should fear,
As they believe twisted half-truths of the utterly, utterly absurd!

Yet we rise above, and follow the Masonic path,
Acting true, exemplary even, as Masons, we all know we should.
Ignore those foolish conspiracies of the ill-informed,
And keep our secrets, helping all we can, in our local neighbourhood!

What is Freemasonry?

Within the lodge, it is a story,
A ritual based on history and fable.
Much like any good book
You may read sitting in your chair or around a table.

Outside the lodge, it is friendship and camaraderie,
A social circle that does good and charitable deeds.
One thing leads to another; when you start you don't stop,
Selfless acts germinating like so many flowering seeds.

We use old-world terms and words, we must declare a faith;
In lodge, politics nor religion are discussed, we treat all with respect.
Despite the conspiracies, and ill-informed nonsense,
We are not dangerous, illicit, illegal; or some dodgy cult or sect!

In short, a network of like-minded individuals
From all walks of life,
Joined by practice of reciting those same old ritual plays,
And a dedication to alleviating others' strife.

A system of morality and symbology,
Private in nature, and much misunderstood.
But know this: to all who would be open, not by conspiracy be blind,
Freemasonry exists, not just for its members, but for the greater good
of mankind!

Is Santa Claus a Mason?

Is Santa Claus a Mason? If so, what colour could his suit be?
Still red? Maybe light, or dark blue, given commitment to the children
every year he'll see?

Is he a founding member, Lodge of the Pole No 1, presiding as the
enduring Master,
Where reindeer and elves are members, making toys, and the sleigh go
faster and faster?

His good wife could be a Lady of the lodge,
Mrs C – supporting with hot chocolate, cookies, and energy-giving stodge.

Santa would make a great ruling Master, leading through example over
the years;
Hard work personified in each annual act, for the good of all children,
Emulated by us, his worthy Masonic peers.

So, if you see glittering sleigh trails in the sky on this Christmas Eve,
Think to yourself, is Santa like me, a Mason, with ritual tucked inside his
sleeve?

And with each present our children open, on every Christmas morn,
Just think to yourself, would Santa also be a Mason?
For on the same principles his conduct seems sworn!

Brethren, I will leave you, on Christmas Eve, with this final thought:
Think on this, use imagination, and believe as we are taught!

Could HO, HO, HO, be a Masonic ritual cry
In the magical degree of the North Pole,
Joined only if you've seen those sleigh trails
across the magical
Festive
And holy
Christmas Eve sky?

LEAD BY EXAMPLE.

SET AN EXAMPLE.

LIVE BY EXAMPLE.

BE
THE EXAMPLE

About the Author

Brother Anthony D. Wilkins

Anthony Wilkins, Ant to his friends, was born and raised in Leicestershire. The son of a farming family, on completion of schooling, he elected to see the world and join the Royal Navy, serving on various ships and Naval Air Squadrons, and attaining the rank of Chief Petty Officer. Married for the second (and final) time to Vanessa, he has three children. He settled in Cornwall towards the end of his Naval career and is now employed by Great Western Railway.

Brother Anthony joined Freemasonry in 2014. As he neared the end of his military career, he was looking for the same kind of camaraderie and belonging he had enjoyed for the entirety of his working life thus far. He thought it was likely he could find this with Freemasonry, through discussion with an old friend and mentor, who also happened to be a Freemason.

Anthony was initiated into Penwith Lodge, meeting in Hayle. Since that time, he has become a member of The Millennium Lodge of Cornwall, aided in creating a University Scheme lodge for the province of Cornwall – Lodge of the Chisel, exalted into St Levan Chapter in Penzance – and advanced into St Michael's Lodge of Mark Master Masons. He will also shortly be joining the Knights Templar Degree.

Anthony has had a passing interest in rhyming poetry since childhood where, as an immature young man, quick rhymes were made up for the amusement of his friends. Now, as a Freemason, he has found an outlet for this creativity and enjoys making rhyming poetry about his passions of Freemasonry, his time in the services, and as a Community Safety Volunteer with the RNLI.

Connect with Anthony on these social media channels:

Youtube: www.youtube.com/channel/
UCfMyZTITbOFj53Ld2vswt_w

Facebook: @MasonicPoet

Twitter: @Masonic_Poet

Instagram: @masonic_poetry

Poet Laureate Robert 'Rabbie' Burns

Bro Robert 'Rabbie' Burns was born on 25th January 1759, the eldest of seven children. He became a Freemason, initiated on 4th July 1781 into St David's Lodge, Tarbolton.

He was subsequently passed to fellowcraft and then raised to the sublime degree of Master Mason on 1st of October 1781. Taking Freemasonry seriously, he joined a total of six lodges during his life.

According to history, there was some dissension and controversy over two lodges at the time: Lodge St David's and St James. Burns eventually went with Lodge St James on 27th July 1784.

Tradition holds that, at one point, he was installed in one lodge as 'Poet Laureate', but this cannot be proven as no records or minutes exist to prove this fact one way or the other.

He rose in Freemasonry, possibly largely due to his creative ability. This was exemplified at a Lodge St Andrew meeting in 1787, where Burns was toasted by the Worshipful Grand Master and Grand Lodge of Scotland present, by the Most Worshipful Brother Francis Chateris with the words, 'Caledonia and Caledonia's Bard, Bro Robert Burns'.

Bro Burns was exalted into the Holy Royal Arch, at St Ebbe's Lodge, Eyemouth in May of 1787.

In 1792, he was elected SW and served one year, the last Masonic office he held before his death on 21st July 1796.

Masonic influence and ideals are present in many works, besides those specific to the craft; some examples, amongst many others identifiable to workers of the craft, are 'Libel Summons', 'A Man's a Man for That' and 'Masonic Song'.

In writings about Robert Burns, Freemasonry, as well as Burns himself, has been credited with speaking out about ideals of liberty, fraternity and equality, and also with being partly responsible for creating feelings of nationalistic pride and fervour, as a number of historic Freemasons played prominent roles in the American and French Revolutions.

Whilst not producing the same feelings per se, in Scotland it did aid in generating a national identity over many years, and indeed generations, by supporting the literary figures such as Burns.

By reading about Bro Robert, you can ascertain he had a fairly rough life, and he appears to have found little solace in the church or society, but Freemasonry remained one of the most important aspects of his life. When all others had abandoned and condemned him, the lodge still welcomed him as a brother.

One poem, the 'Farewell' to his brothers at St James Lodge, expressed a sincere sadness at leaving Scotland for Jamaica. Many speculate that his brothers' support in lodge convinced him to reconsider his position and stay. After this low point, he went on to produce some of his greatest works.

Above all else, Freemasonry's spirit of brotherhood is ensconced in his creations. Those who are privileged to be members of the craft can spot the Masonic influence.

Aside from 'Ode to the Haggis', heard by many in the UK and across the world who have knowledge of and attend Burns Night dinners, the most well-known poems are plentiful, but arguably none more so than the poem and song 'Auld Lang Syne'.

'Auld Lang Syne' is sung planet-wide by many religions and denominations, including those who do not have faith, but accept the ideals of decency towards all humankind, and this song resonates with the message from Burns' heart of old friends reminiscing about days past. T. G. Patterson said that 'Auld Lang Syne' is a concrete expression of his love for all mankind and his ideal of international brotherhood.